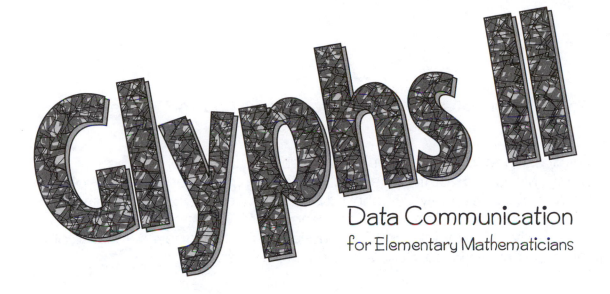

Glyphs II

Data Communication
for Elementary Mathematicians

by Susan R. O'Connell

Good Apple
A Division of Frank Schaffer Publications, Inc.

Dedicated to
Gail Naworal for her ability to inspire, support, and encourage
students and teachers

Thanks to the following teachers at Glenn Dale Elementary School in Prince George's County, Maryland, for their help in field testing the glyphs in this book: Nancy Snyder, Nancy Jones, Kelly O'Connor, Lisa Hazel, David Dove, Joy Bishop, Maureen Cassidy, Curt Hefflin, Sandi Lanham, Angie Terry, Liz Haney, Sallie Smith, Ann Blackwood, Jody Mackowiak, and Rosemarie McConnaughey. And special thanks to Joanie and Dave Pinson for their computer expertise.

Editor: Donna Garzinsky
Designers: Joe Galka
          Lisa Ann Arcuri
Cover: Lisa Ann Arcuri

Good Apple
A Division of Frank Schaffer Publications, Inc.
23740 Hawthorne Boulevard
Torrance, CA 90505-5927

ISBN: 1-56417-901-X

    5 6 7 8 9   01 00

Contents

Introduction

What are glyphs?

Glyphs are becoming the exciting new way for elementary students to collect, display, and interpret data. Taken from the ancient hieroglyphics, glyphs are a way of pictorially representing data. Students create pictures, with each part of the picture representing a unique bit of information. In facial glyphs the shape of the eyes might represent the number of children in a student's family. The expression of the mouth might represent the age of the child. And the hair (curly or straight) might represent the student's handedness. This unique blend of art and data analysis has made glyphs a creative data analysis technique that has excited students in many classrooms throughout the country.

Why use glyphs with elementary students?

The *National Council of Teachers of Mathematics*, in their "Curriculum and Evaluation Standards for School Mathematics," places emphasis on data analysis. Teachers are encouraged to provide students with a variety of experiences collecting, displaying, and interpreting data.

Glyph activities begin with the collection of data. This is done by means of a survey. In many cases, students gather data about their own lives, making the task particularly meaningful to them. They then follow a series of directions to display the data they've collected. The pictures that are created represent that data. Once the glyphs are created, there are many exciting ways that students can analyze and interpret the glyphs. In the process of exploring their glyphs, students are provided opportunities to communicate their mathematical thinking both orally and in writing.

Glyphs help to build students' data-analysis and communication skills as they write and talk about their data. Glyphs also stimulate students' mathematical reasoning as they compare, contrast, and draw conclusions from their data. Glyphs provide students opportunities to apply previously learned mathematics skills, such as using a ruler to measure the length of streamers in

the Shamrock Mobile Glyph (p. 49), using their knowledge of shapes to add facial features to their Jack-o'-lantern Glyphs (p. 25), demonstrating their knowledge of fractions when shading 3/4 of a window on their My Home Glyphs (p. 65), or using a compass to construct circles for their Who Am I? Glyphs (p. 16). And most importantly, glyphs create excitement and add fun to your mathematics classroom!

How should glyph activities be introduced to students?

Students who are unfamiliar with glyphs will benefit from a step-by-step approach. To introduce glyph-making, use an overhead projector, chalkboard, or easel. Choose one glyph activity to do as an example. Draw or post the selected glyph shape for students to see. Read aloud each survey question, adding your own picture detail to the glyph shape after each question. Seeing the glyph being made will help students understand the construction process. After students have heard all the survey questions and watched you use your answers to create a glyph, the students will be ready to begin their own glyphs. Provide students with

appropriate construction materials. Go back to the first survey question, reread it to the class, and allow students time to construct the first part of their glyphs. Proceed slowly in this manner, offering assistance as needed. (Many teachers prefer to take the sample glyph away at this time so that students do not duplicate the sample.)

You may wish to allow students who have previous experience constructing glyphs to independently read the survey questions and circle their answers. Provide the needed supplies and students can then proceed at their own pace to construct the glyphs, following the glyph directions. Briefly show a sample to allow students to visualize the end product before beginning their glyphs. This will help answer design or construction questions that students may have.

Why is it important to do additional activities once the glyphs have been created?

Answering survey questions and representing the data on glyphs are only the beginning of what glyphs can teach students. After collecting and representing the data, provide students with opportunities to

interpret, analyze, and communicate about the data. Encourage students to look at classmates' glyphs and make statements about the data ("Brendan likes baseball best"); find similarities and differences between students' glyphs ("Nori likes fruit in her cereal, but Ivan doesn't"); and draw conclusions from the data collected ("Everyone in our class . . ." or "No one likes . . . "). Students will benefit from opportunities to practice communicating about the glyph information to partners, groups, and the entire class, and from expressing their ideas in writing. Most of all, give students an opportunity to share their glyphs and their survey answers with classmates.

Note: Various graphing activities are included with several of the glyphs (see pp. 20, 24, 25, 30, 34, 35, 41, 43, 53, 56, 59–61, 64, and 80). For more information on graphs and how to use them, you may wish to consult *Used Numbers—Statistics: Middles, Means, and In-Betweens* by Susan N. Friel, Janice R. Mokros, and Susan Jo Russell (Dale Seymour Publications, California, 1992), *Data, Chance & Probability* by Graham A. Jones and Carol A. Thornton (Learning Resources, Illinois, 1993), or *Exploring Data* by James M. Landwehr and Ann E. Watkins (Dale Seymour Publications, California, 1986).

How can glyph activities be modified to meet the needs of a specific group of students?

Before beginning any glyph with your class, read the glyph instructions and survey-directions ahead of time to be sure that students have the mathematics skills needed to complete the glyph. In many cases a quick review of the skill, such as measurement, identification of shapes, or fractions may be all that is needed to allow students to successfully complete the glyph. Glyphs can easily be modified if a question appears too difficult for your students. For example, if students have not mastered measuring to a fraction of an inch, white out the football laces' dimensions on the survey-directions page in the Football Glyph (p. 31) and replace them with measurements to the nearest inch. If measuring to the nearest inch is too easy for your class, change the measurements to fractions of an inch or use the metric measurements provided for many of the glyphs to challenge students.

Another modification would be to precut some items and have students select the correct size. In the TV Time Glyph, you would cut out three sizes of rectangles that

match the three measurements listed. Students who do not yet have the skills necessary to construct the rectangles to the correct size may be able to measure the precut paper and select the correct size.

For glyphs that involve measuring, two reproducible pages are provided—one with U.S. measurements and one with metric measurements. This will allow you to select the measurement system you wish to use or focus on for the day's lesson.

How can students add their own creative touches to the glyphs?

The glyphs in this book are designed for easy classroom use, with reproducible patterns supplied for most of the glyphs. The glyphs, however, can be made more creative by allowing students to design their own patterns on colorful construction paper. For example, in the Jack-o'-lantern (p. 25) or Football Glyphs (p. 30), students may begin their glyphs by drawing their own pumpkins or footballs. Read the directions carefully when selecting paper for students' glyphs, since paper color is sometimes a factor in designing the glyphs. Use thicker paper, such as construction paper or

posterboard, when students will be sharing or displaying the glyphs. Students may also show their creativity and personal touch by designing additional survey questions to add to their glyphs. These questions, however, should be shared with the class so that the glyphs can be accurately interpreted. Be sure that students do not make their glyphs difficult to interpret by adding too many creative touches. Creating an accurate glyph based on the survey data and being able to interpret that data are the ultimate goals.

Should parents be included in glyph activities?

Yes! When parents are familiar with glyphs and why we use them, they are better able to help their children. The Birthday Gift Glyph, a parent-child glyph found on page 12, should be sent home when you are introducing glyphs to your class. Along with providing a reinforcement lesson, the take-home glyph explains glyphs to parents and offers them a hands-on way of learning about glyphs by creating glyphs with their child. Another parent-child glyph (Postage Stamp Glyph, p. 73) is included for an additional home project. Parent involvement is

recommended for the Postage Stamp Glyph, since data collection involves sorting and counting the family's mail each day. However, any of the glyphs in this book can be sent home as enjoyable, interactive projects for parents and children. Helping parents become aware of what glyphs are and how they help students explore data will give them the knowledge they need to reinforce classroom lessons and assist their children at home. For your convenience, a sample reproducible letter to families is provided on page 11.

What materials are needed to create glyphs?

The first page of each glyph activity lists the materials needed for each student to create a glyph as well as the supplies needed for the additional activities. In general, these materials may include construction, writing, and graph paper; posterboard; pens, pencils, markers, and crayons; scissors; glue; tape; compasses; protractors; rulers; calculators; and math journals (if desired). Access to a photocopier to reproduce glyph patterns and worksheets will also be needed.

How can teachers assess students' understanding of glyphs?

In assessing students' understanding of glyphs, several factors must be considered.

- Are students able to accurately create glyphs from a set of data?

- Are students able to interpret data by looking at a completed glyph?

- Are students able to communicate about glyph data?

In assessing students' ability to accurately create glyphs, ask students to circle their survey responses. Then check each student's glyph against his or her survey to be sure that the student has accurately represented the data. In scoring mathematics performance tasks, many teachers prefer a scoring key similar to the one below, as opposed to traditional grading methods. With this key, students are evaluated on the degree to which they are able to perform the task.

3—All of the data is accurately represented on the glyph.

2—Most of the data is accurately represented on the glyph.

1—Some of the data is accurately represented on the glyph.

0—None of the data is accurately represented on the glyph.

Offering students opportunities to write about their glyphs will provide feedback on their understanding of the glyph activities. Assessments, however, do not

---

Bookmark Glyph

1. Where do you read more?

	school	home
add a border with	wavy lines	straight lines

2. Do you like to read in bed?

	yes	no
divide bookmark lengthwise with a	wavy line	straight line

3. About how many books do you read each month?

	0	1	2	3	4	5 . . .
number of circles	0	1	2	3	4	5 . . .

4. Of the following types of books, which would you rather read?

	mystery	biography	nonfiction	humor
number of triangles	1	2	3	4

5. How many times do you go to the library each month?

	0	1 or 2	3 or more
number of squares	0	1 or 2	3

62

© 1997 Good Apple

Sample Assessment

(based on the Bookmark Glyph on page 62)

Brenda   Melissa   José   Steven   Tyrell   Marcella   Kira

Look at the Bookmark Glyphs shown above to answer the following questions.

1. Which students like to read in bed?_____

_____

2. Explain how you know this. _____

_____

3. Complete the line plot to show about how many books these students read each month.

0   1   2   3   4   5   6   7   8

Which student reads the most?_____
Which student reads the least?_____

4. Which type of book do most students prefer?_____

5. Explain how you know this. _____

_____

80

© 1997 Good Apple

When assessing students' ability to interpret glyphs, you may wish to use some of the glyphs created by the class or develop your own written assessment tasks. A sample task based on the Bookmark Glyph (see p. 61) is shown on page 80 and in reduced form above. In this assessment task, students are asked to look at some glyphs and answer questions about the data that is represented on each one.

have to be written tasks. Many of the additional activities presented in this book can be used for assessment. You might observe group work, assess Venn diagrams, or observe students to see that glyphs are correctly grouped or sorted. Whether it is through a formal assessment task or an informal observation, assessment should be ongoing to monitor student understanding and progress.

Concepts and Skills Chart

For your convenience the chart below lists the concepts and skills utilized to create each glyph and explore its additional activities.

	Reasoning	Problem Solving	Communications	Connections	Data Analysis	Measurement	Geometry	Fractions	Probability	Statistics	Map Skills
Name Tag Glyph	X	X	X	X	X						
Who Am I? Glyph	X	X	X	X	X	X	X				
TV Time Glyph	X	X	X	X	X	X	X				
Jack-o'-lantern Glyph	X	X	X	X	X	X	X				
Football Glyph	X	X	X	X	X	X				X	
Cereal Box Glyph	X	X	X	X	X		X				
Off We Go! Glyph	X	X	X	X	X		X	X			X
Cookie Glyph	X	X	X	X	X					X	
Fun and Games Glyph	X	X	X	X	X	X		X	X		
Shamrock Mobile Glyph	X	X	X	X	X	X	X	X			
Weather Watchers Glyph	X	X	X	X	X	X					
Play Ball! Glyph	X	X	X	X	X	X	X	X			
Bookmark Glyph	X	X	X	X	X		X			X	
My Home Glyph	X	X	X	X	X	X	X	X			X
Super Sandwich Glyph	X	X	X	X	X	X					
Postage Stamp Glyph	X	X	X	X	X					X	

Dear Family,

We are learning about glyphs in math class. A glyph is a way to represent information in picture or graphic form. Like the ancient hieroglyphics, glyphs represent data pictorially. Each part of the picture represents a piece of information.

I am enclosing a glyph for you to do with your child. You'll need a pencil, the glyph survey-directions, and two sheets of paper to complete the activity. Ask your child to read the glyph survey questions and then write down or circle his or her answers. Next, based on those answers, have your child create a birthday gift glyph by following the directions on the survey page. The shape of the box, the ribbon and bow, and the pattern on the wrapping paper will be determined by your child's answers to the survey questions.

After your child's glyph is completed, use the second sheet of paper to make a glyph reflecting your answers. When done, ask your child to make some statements about you by looking at your glyph. Then have him or her compare the two glyphs to find out what you share in common and how you are different.

Glyphs can help students gather information, display information in graphic form, and interpret information. Some glyphs are easy, while others challenge students by asking them to measure with rulers, construct circles with compasses, and draw angles using protractors. Glyphs help students apply some of the math skills they've learned in class, plus they're lots of fun! Thank you for helping your child understand glyphs. If you have any questions, please do not hesitate to call.

Sincerely,

_____

Birthday Gift Glyph

1. Which birthday dessert do you like best?

	cake	ice cream
shape of package	square	rectangle

2. Would you rather celebrate your birthday with a big party or a quiet celebration?

	big party	small celebration
add ribbon		

3. On your next birthday will you have . . .

	12 or fewer candles on your cake	more than 12 candles
add a bow?	yes	no

4. In which month of the year were you born?

	Jan.–Mar.	Apr.–Jun.	Jul.–Sept.	Oct.–Dec.
decorate package with	squares	triangles	circles	hearts

5. Do you prefer birthday cards that are handmade or store-bought?

	handmade	store-bought
shade ribbon with pencil?	yes	no

12

Name Tag Glyph

This "getting to know you" glyph activity is perfect for the start of the school year. Invite students to create Name Tag Glyphs by answering questions about themselves. (See the survey on p. 14). The completed glyphs can then be taped to students' desks, if desired, to help students and teacher get to know one another.

Materials

- ❖ glyph survey-directions
- ❖ name tag pattern
- ❖ crayons or markers
- ❖ tape

Additional Activities

⟳ Collect all the glyphs. Mix the glyphs up and give each student a glyph, making sure it is not his or her own. Ask each student to introduce the person whose glyph he or she is holding. By looking at the glyph for information, students should be able to share some facts about the person. After all the children are introduced, the Name Tag Glyphs can be taped to students' desks.

⟳ For Back-to-School Night, post a copy of the glyph survey questions and directions on the bulletin board or chalkboard for parents to use to interpret the Name Tag Glyphs that have been taped to desks.

⟳ Information from the glyphs can be used to design a birthday graph or chart for the class. Have students sort the glyphs by month and then arrange them by date.

Teacher Note

Remind students to read all the survey questions before beginning to construct their glyphs. Questions #1 and #2 both contain information about how students' names should be written on the Name Tag Glyphs.

Name Tag Glyph

1. What is your position in your family?

	oldest	youngest	middle	only
write name in	black	green	red	blue

2. Are you new to this school or did you go here last year?

	new	was here last year
write name in	cursive	printing (manuscript)

3. In which month were you born?

Draw a design on your name tag.

January—snowman	July—sailboat
February—heart	August—sun
March—kite	September—apple
April—umbrella	October—pumpkin
May—flower	November—leaf
June—fish	December—tree

4. On which day of the month were you born?

	1st	2nd	3rd	4th	5th . . .	31st
number of dots on border	1	2	3	4	5 . . .	31

5. How many brothers and sisters do you have?

	0	1	2	3	4 or more
color of border	green	blue	purple	yellow	red

14

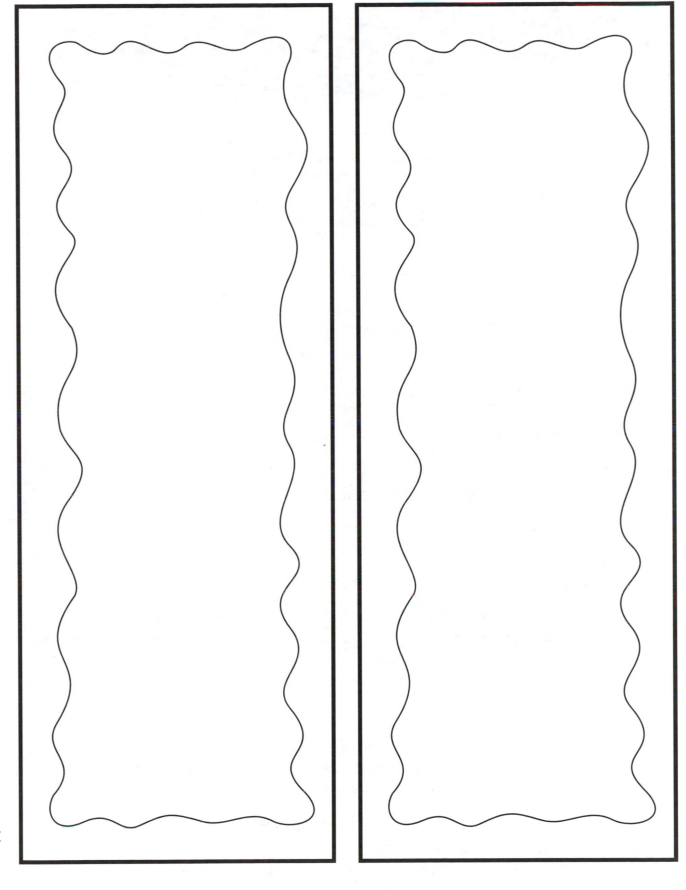

Who Am I? Glyph

Invite students to create owl glyphs by answering the survey questions on page 17 or 18 about their first names. Compasses are used to construct circular eyes, and protractors are used to create beaks with specific angles. You may wish to review these skills with the class before beginning this glyph.

Materials

- ❖ glyph survey-directions
- ❖ owl pattern
- ❖ crayons or markers
- ❖ protractor
- ❖ compass

Additional Activities

List all the students' first names on the chalkboard. Then invite students to play a guessing game with the completed glyphs.

- Have students label the backs of their glyphs with their initials, names, or created symbols that they would recognize.

- Mix up the glyphs and give one to each student.

- Ask students to decode the information represented on the glyphs to guess whose glyph they are holding. (Although the clues will eliminate many names, there may be several names that fit all the data on a glyph. A student would then need to guess whose glyph he or she is holding from the possible choices.)

Teacher Notes

In question #1, if students are not able to use compasses yet, substitute *shape of eyes* for *radius of eyes*, offering the choices of *round* or *oval*.

In question #3, if protractors cannot be used, substitute *color of beak* for *angle of beak*. Allow students to draw their own beaks or, if you prefer, draw a beak on the owl pattern before duplicating. Offer four different color choices.

Who Am I? Glyph

1. Does your first name begin with a consonant or a vowel?

	consonant	vowel
radius of eyes	$\frac{1}{2}$"	

2. How many letters are in your first name?

	2–4	5–7	8 or more
design of eyes	⊙ ⊙	◠ ◠	◑ ◑

3. Does your first name begin with . . .

	a–f	g–l	m–r	s–z
angle of beak	40°	50°	60°	70°

4. Are there more consonants, more vowels, or the same number of each in your first name?

	more consonants	more vowels	same
claws	⋀⋀	⋀⋀	⋁⋁

5. How many syllables are in your first name?

	1	2	3 or more
triangle	▽	▽	▽

U.S. measurement

Who Am I? Glyph

1. Does your first name begin with a consonant or a vowel?

	consonant	vowel
radius of eyes	1.5 cm	2 cm

2. How many letters are in your first name?

	2–4	5–7	8 or more
design of eyes	⊙ ⊙	⊖ ⊖	⌣ ⌣

3. Does your first name begin with . . .

	a–f	g–l	m–r	s–z
angle of beak	40°	50°	60°	70°

4. Are there more consonants, more vowels, or the same number of each in your first name?

	more consonants	more vowels	same
claws	ᗱᗴ	ᗽᗽ	ᐯᐯ

5. How many syllables are in your first name?

	1	2	3 or more
triangle	▽	▽	▽

Metric measurement

18

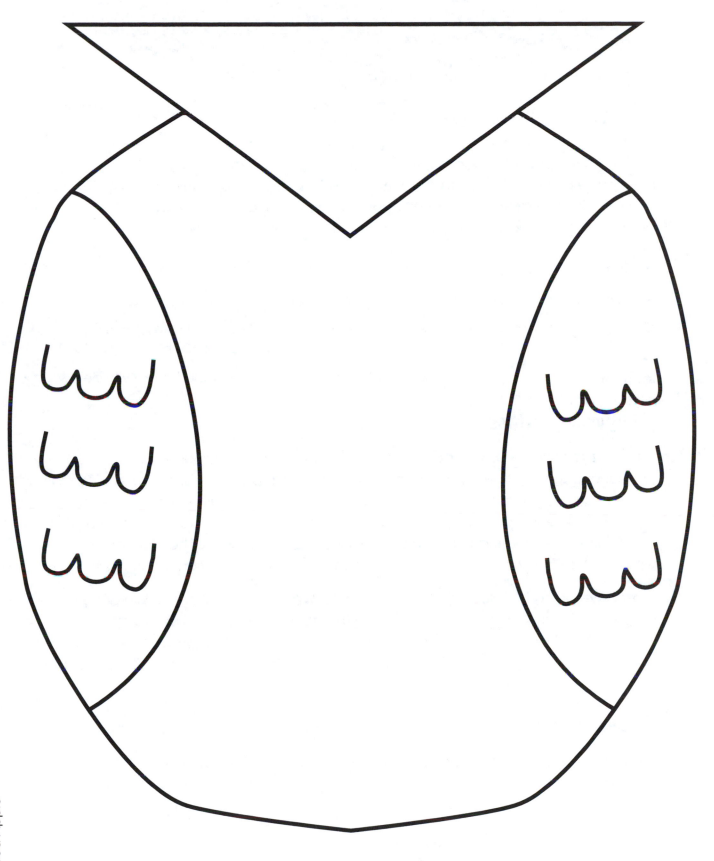

TV Time Glyph

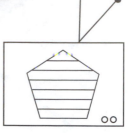

Invite students to create TV Time Glyphs as they answer survey questions about their television-viewing habits. Advise students to begin drawing their TV shapes near the bottoms of their papers. If needed, a pattern to help students make the TV rectangle is included on page 23. You may wish to review how to construct angles with a protractor, as this skill is needed to construct the "rabbit ear" antennae.

Materials

- ❖ glyph survey and directions
- ❖ paper or pattern on page 23
- ❖ pencil
- ❖ ruler
- ❖ protractor
- ❖ Comparison of Daily TV Viewing Hours worksheet, on page 24 (for activity below)
- ❖ tape, paper, and pencil (for activity below)

Additional Activities

Label five areas of the chalkboard or bulletin board with the headings *0, 1, 2, 3,* and *4 or more.* Ask students to tape their glyphs under the correct heading based on the hours of TV watched on an average weekday. After tallying and recording the number of glyphs under each heading, have students repeat the process for weekend days. Students can then use the information collected to create a double bar graph showing the amount of hours that classmates watched television on weekends compared to weekdays (see worksheet on p. 24).

After developing the class graph described above, ask students to work in groups to create problems that can be solved using the double bar graph. For example, what is the average number of hours that students watched TV on weekdays? weekend days? Have groups switch problems and solve the other's problems. Students can write or explain how they solved the problems.

Teacher Notes

If students are unable to construct angles using a protractor (see survey question #4), you may wish to substitute *color of buttons* for *angle of antennae*, offering four color choices.

TV Time Glyph

1. What is your favorite time of day to watch TV?

	morning	afternoon	evening
size of TV (h x w)	$4\frac{1}{2}"$ x $6\frac{1}{2}"$	$5\frac{1}{2}"$ x $6\frac{1}{2}"$	$6\frac{1}{2}"$ x $6\frac{1}{2}"$

2. About how many hours do you spend watching TV on a typical weekday? Estimate to the nearest hour.

	0	1	2	3	4 or more
shape of screen	rectangle	square	octagon	hexagon	pentagon

3. About how many hours do you spend watching TV on a typical weekend day (Saturday or Sunday)? Estimate to the nearest hour.

	0	1	2	3	4 or more
# of buttons	0	1	2	3	4

4. What is your favorite type of television show?

	sitcom	cartoons (animated)	drama	other
angle of antennae	20°	30°	40°	50°

5. Would you rather watch TV, read a book, or play a game?

	watch TV	read a book	play a game
design on screen	horizontal lines	vertical lines	no design

U.S. measurement

TV Time Glyph

1. What is your favorite time of day to watch TV?

	morning	afternoon	evening
size of TV (h x w)	11 cm x 16.5 cm	13 cm x 16.5 cm	15 cm x 16.5 cm

2. About how many hours do you spend watching TV on a typical weekday? Estimate to the nearest hour.

	0	1	2	3	4 or more
shape of screen	rectangle	square	octagon	hexagon	pentagon

3. About how many hours do you spend watching TV on a typical weekend day (Saturday or Sunday)? Estimate to the nearest hour.

	0	1	2	3	4 or more
# of buttons	0	1	2	3	4

4. What is your favorite type of television show?

	sitcom	cartoons (animated)	drama	other
angle of antennae	20°	30°	40°	50°

5. Would you rather watch TV, read a book, or play a game?

	watch TV	read a book	play a game
design on screen	horizontal lines	vertical lines	no design

Metric measurement

22

This pattern provides the bottom lines of a TV. Students can add side and top lines by measuring the correct lengths and drawing in the lines.

23

Name_____ Date_____

Comparison of Daily TV Viewing Hours
Weekday vs. Weekend

Tally

Hours	Weekdays	Weekends
0		
1		
2		
3		
4 or more		

Double Bar Graph

Color Code
- ☐ weekdays
- ☐ weekends

_____
(title)

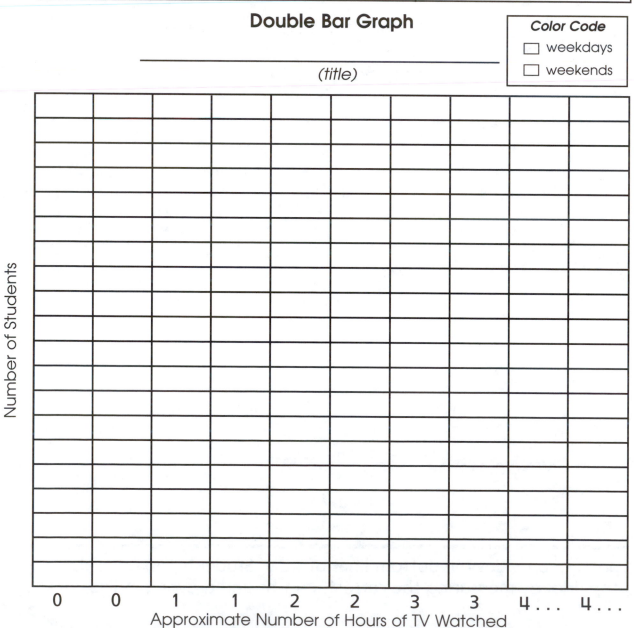

Number of Students

0   0   1   1   2   2   3   3   4 . . .   4 . . .

Approximate Number of Hours of TV Watched

Students will enjoy creating Jack-o'-lantern Glyphs. First have students either draw on construction paper pumpkin shapes with no stems or provide copies of the pumpkin pattern on page 28. Then ask students to answer the survey questions about pumpkins and autumn to determine the features to add to their jack-o'-lanterns.

Materials

- ❖ glyph survey-directions
- ❖ pumpkin pattern or construction paper
- ❖ rulers
- ❖ crayons or markers
- ❖ triple Venn diagram on posterboard (for activity below)

- ❖ scissors and tape (for activity below)
- ❖ math journals and pens or pencils (for activity below)
- ❖ Venn diagram worksheet, on page 29 (for activity below)

Additional Activities

⊚ Have students work in groups of four to six. Provide each group with a large triple Venn diagram on a piece of posterboard. Have the groups label the three circles *Likes pumpkin pie*, *Likes scary jack-o'-lanterns*, and *Candy corn is favorite fall treat*. Ask students to work together to decide where to place their pumpkins on the diagram. Have students cut out and tape their glyphs on the diagrams and then present the diagrams to the class. Ask students to write in their math journals what their diagram shows.

⊚ Have students work in groups of three to compare their glyphs. Using a triple Venn diagram (see worksheet on p. 29), have students compare the three glyphs and record the ways that the three students are alike and different.

⊚ Ask students to create bar graphs to show the class's favorite kind of jack-o'-lantern. Have students tally and graph the data from survey question #3. Students can then write about what their bar graphs show.

Jack-o'-lantern Glyph

1. Have you ever eaten pumpkin seeds?

	yes	no
draw a stem with this height	1"	$\frac{3}{4}$"

2. Do you like pumpkin pie?

	yes	no	don't know
mouth			

3. Do you like scary or happy jack-o'-lanterns?

	scary	happy
nose	square	triangle

4. Which fall treat do you prefer?

	caramel apples	popcorn balls	candy corn	pumpkin pie
eyes	octagons	pentagons	hexagons	circles

5. Have you ever eaten pumpkin bread?

	yes	no
draw vine from stem with	1 loop	2 loops

Now color your pumpkin.

U.S. measurement

26

Jack-o'-lantern Glyph

1. Have you ever eaten pumpkin seeds?

	yes	no
draw a stem with this height	25 mm	20 mm

2. Do you like pumpkin pie?

	yes	no	don't know
mouth			

3. Do you like scary or happy jack-o'-lanterns?

	scary	happy
nose	square	triangle

4. Which fall treat do you prefer?

	caramel apples	popcorn balls	candy corn	pumpkin pie
eyes	octagons	pentagons	hexagons	circles

5. Have you ever eaten pumpkin bread?

	yes	no
draw vine from stem with	1 loop	2 loops

Now color your pumpkin.

Metric measurement

28

Comparing Jack-o'-lantern Glyphs

Using the data from your Jack-o'-lantern Glyphs, fill in the Venn diagram below with ways you and your partners are alike and ways that you are different. Label each circle with a student's name.

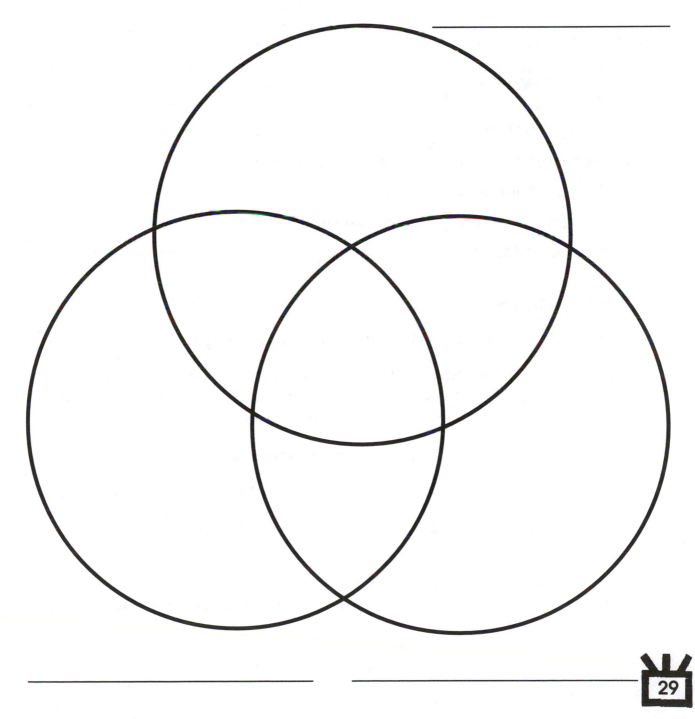

_____ _____

Football Glyph

Invite students to answer questions about the game of football to create Football Glyphs. The completed glyphs can be used to gather data for a class pictograph.

Materials

❖ glyph survey-directions

❖ football pattern

❖ ruler

❖ crayons or markers

❖ sports section of a discarded newspaper (for activity below)

❖ math journal (for activity below)

❖ plain or graph paper (for activity below)

❖ Which Football Skill Is Easiest? worksheet, on page 34 (for activity below)

Additional Activities

⊚ Display the glyphs on a bulletin board or chalkboard ledge.

- Pair students and ask each pair to create a pictograph or complete the graph in the Which Football Skill Is Easiest? worksheet to show the class's responses to survey question #3 (*Do you think it's easier to throw, kick, or catch a football?*).

- Have students write about what the graph data shows.

⊚ Invite students to find football statistics in the sports section of a newspaper.

- Have students prepare a graph to show the number of wins for each professional sports team.

- Students could also prepare a double bar graph showing the wins and losses for selected teams, or team wins at home vs. team wins on the road.

Football Glyph

1. Do you like to watch football on TV?

	yes	no
length of laces ⬭—	$1\frac{3}{4}"$	$2\frac{1}{4}"$

2. Do you own any clothing that has the name of a football team or player on it?

	yes	no
design of laces	⬭+++	⬭✳✳✳

3. Do you think it's easier to . . .

	throw a football	kick a football	catch a football
stripes	⬭	⬭	⬭

4. Have you been to a college or professional football game?

	yes	no
logo on ball	star	lightning bolt

5. If a football game was on TV, would you rather watch the game or the halftime show?

	game	halftime show
color of ball	brown	orange

U.S. measurement

Football Glyph

1. Do you like to watch football on TV?

		yes	no
length of laces	⬭	44 mm	57 mm

2. Do you own any clothing that has the name of a football team or player on it?

	yes	no
design of laces	⬭ ⧾⧾⧾	⬭ ✕✕✕

3. Do you think it's easier to . . .

	throw a football	kick a football	catch a football
stripes	⬭	⬭	⬭

4. Have you been to a college or professional football game?

	yes	no
logo on ball	star	lightning bolt

5. If a football game was on TV, would you rather watch the game or the halftime show?

	game	halftime show
color of ball	brown	orange

Metric measurement

32

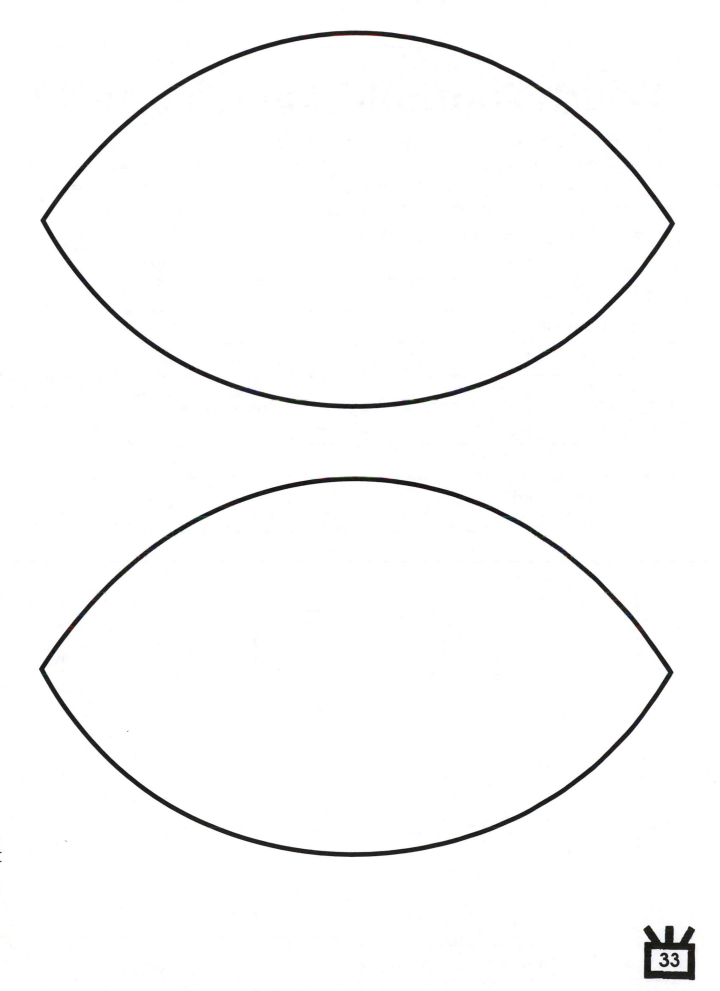

Which Football Skill Is Easiest?

1. Look at the class's completed football glyphs. Place a tally mark in the tally sheet below to show each student's response to question #3 (*Do you think it's easier to throw a football, kick a football, or catch a football?*). Then add up the tally marks and write the totals in the column on the right.

	Total number of tally marks
throw a football	
kick a football	
catch a football	

2. Which part of the glyphs shows the students' responses to question #3?

_____

3. Complete the pictograph below to show your class's answers. Each football stands for two students.

_____   = 2 students
(*pictograph title*)

throw   kick   catch

Cereal Box Glyph

Invite students to create Cereal Box Glyphs, using their answers to the survey on page 36. You may wish to review with students the terms *vertical*, *horizontal*, and *diagonal* before beginning this glyph.

Materials

❖ glyph survey-directions

❖ cereal box pattern

❖ pencil

❖ math journal (for activity below)

❖ Cereal Box Scavenger Hunt worksheet, on page 37 (for activity below)

❖ markers (for activity below)

Additional Activities

◎ Send students on a silent Cereal Box Scavenger Hunt (see worksheet on p. 37).

- Have students write their names on their glyphs, then place the glyphs on their desks.

- Provide students with copies of the worksheet. Ask children to walk around the room, filling in the worksheet blanks with students' names as they find glyphs that match the directions. Have students return to their seats as they individually finish the worksheet. When most students are done, ask students to correct the worksheets by calling out each direction and having students stand if their glyphs match the information given.

◎ Have students create a class graph showing the number of students who like fruit in their cereal and those who prefer no fruit in their cereal. Ask students to write in their math journals, describing the graph's data.

◎ Students may also enjoy adding color to their completed glyphs.

Cereal Box Glyph

1. Would you rather eat cereal with or without milk?

	milk	no milk
write the word *cereal* diagonally in the center of your cereal box using	all capital letters	all lowercase letters

2. When is your favorite time to eat cereal?

	morning	afternoon	evening
draw in top triangle			

3. Do you like fruit in your cereal?

	yes	no
draw in bottom triangle		

4. How many days each week do you eat cereal?

	0–1	2–3	4–5	6–7
design on bowl	vertical lines	horizontal lines	dots	stars

5. Is your favorite cereal round, square, or another shape?

	round	square	other
fill bowl with shapes	circles	squares	triangles

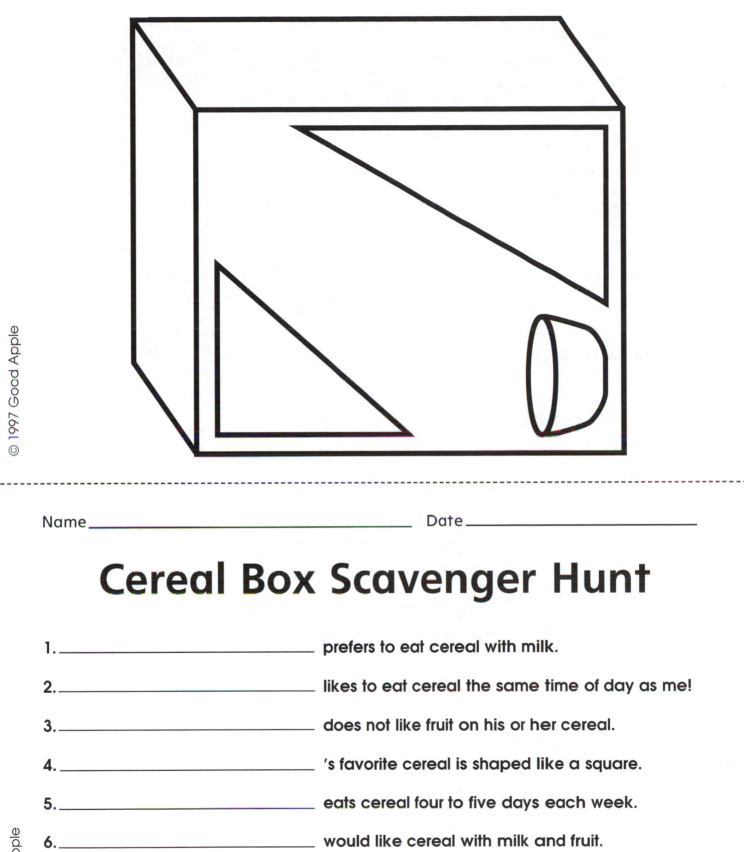

Name_____ Date_____

Cereal Box Scavenger Hunt

1. _____ prefers to eat cereal with milk.

2. _____ likes to eat cereal the same time of day as me!

3. _____ does not like fruit on his or her cereal.

4. _____ 's favorite cereal is shaped like a square.

5. _____ eats cereal four to five days each week.

6. _____ would like cereal with milk and fruit.

Off We Go! Glyph

Invite students to answer survey questions about their dream vacations to create luggage glyphs.

Materials

- glyph survey-directions
- luggage pattern
- crayons or markers
- paper and pencil
- map of the United States (for activity below)
- research materials such as encyclopedias (for activity below)

Additional Activities

 Post signs labeled *North*, *South*, *East*, and *West* in the four corners of the room.

- Ask each student to go to the corner that fits his or her answer to question #1.

- Have students compare their glyphs with those of other students in their corner and select a partner or partners based on the similarity of their glyphs. Partners' glyphs should look alike in as many ways as possible.

- Using a map of the United States, have student partners plan a trip to a city that is in the area of the country represented by their glyphs.

- Encourage students to research their cities to decide on fun places to visit.

- Ask students to either determine the distance they will be traveling (by using a map scale) or the cost of getting to their location and back again. (Those traveling by car will need to figure the approximate cost of gas, miles traveled, and typical miles-per-gallon figures. Train, bus, and plane travelers can find the cost for tickets to their destination.)

 Have students report back to the class on their trip plans.

 For an added challenge, have students work in groups to plan trips to other parts of the world, such as Canada, Brazil, England, or Japan.

Off We Go! Glyph

1. Which part of the United States would you like to visit?

	North	South	East	West
shape of handle				

2. How would you get there?

	airplane	train	car	bus
color of handle	green	blue	red	orange

3. When would you go?

	winter	spring	summer	fall
design your luggage with lines that are	parallel and horizontal	parallel and vertical	parallel and diagonal	intersecting

4. Whom would you take with you?

	friends	family	both
wheels on luggage divided into	fourths	sixths	eighths

5. How long would you like to stay?

	1 day	1 week	1 month
luggage color	red	blue	green

Cookie Glyph

Students will enjoy using the information from the nutritional labels of their favorite cookies to create Cookie Glyphs. Ask students to bring packaging labels containing the nutrition information of their preferred cookies to class.

Materials

- ❖ glyph survey and directions
- ❖ nutritional label from favorite brand of cookies (may be shared with a partner if desired)
- ❖ paper plate or 8" (20 cm) circle cut from construction paper
- ❖ crayons or markers
- ❖ pencil or pen (for activity below)
- ❖ Our Class's Cookie Glyph Line Plot worksheet, on page 43 (for activity below)
- ❖ writing paper or math journal (for activity below)

Additional Activities

🌀 Using glyph data, have students create a line plot using the worksheet on page 43 to show the total grams of fat in the cookies chosen by the class. When the line plots are completed, have students each write two conclusions they can draw from the data.

🌀 Ask students to use their line plots to determine the mean, median, mode, and range for their set of data.

🌀 Students could also create line plots showing the total grams of fiber, carbohydrates, protein, cholesterol, or sodium.

🌀 Correlate the cookie glyphs with a health unit on nutrition.

- Ask students to research the effect of fat on the body.

- Based on their research, invite students to create a list of recommended cookies and a list of cookies to avoid.

- Let students explain how they chose cookies for each list.

Cookie Glyph

1. How many cookies are in one serving?

	1	2	3	4 or more
draw this number of cookies	1	2	3	4 . . .

2. How many grams of sugar are in one serving?

	0–5 g	6–10 g	11–15 g	6 g or more
number of chips in each cookie	1	2	3	4

3. How many total grams of fat are in one serving?

	1 g	2 g	3 g	4 g	5 g . . .
number of notches around edge of plate	1	2	3	4	5 . . .

4. When you have cookies for a snack, do you eat 1 serving or more?

	1 serving	2 servings	more than 2 servings	don't eat cookies
color of cookies	orange	yellow	brown	green

Our Class's Cookie Glyph Line Plot

1. Place an *x* by the number of grams of fat shown on each student's cookie glyph.

```
_____
0  1  2  3  4  5  6  7  8  9  10  11  12  13  14  15  16  17
```

2. Write two conclusions you can draw about your class's favorite cookies by looking at the line plot.

A. _____

_____

_____

_____

B. _____

_____

_____

_____

3. Use the data on the line plot to find the following.

mean _____ **median** _____ **mode** _____ **range** _____

Fun and Games Glyph

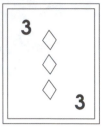

Invite students to create glyphs resembling playing cards by answering survey questions about their favorite games. You may wish to begin the lesson by asking students to brainstorm a list of their favorite games. Students can then sort the games into categories such as card games, ballgames, video games, board games, and any other types of games that are mentioned. This will focus students' thoughts on the types of games they enjoy. Students can then construct their Fun and Games Glyphs.

Materials

- ❖ glyph survey-directions
- ❖ playing-card pattern
- ❖ ruler
- ❖ scissors
- ❖ crayons or markers

- ❖ pencil or pen (for activity below)
- ❖ Fun and Games Probability worksheet on page 48 (for activity below)
- ❖ math journal (for activity below)

Additional Activities

🌀 Using the glyph data, ask students to make a class tally of favorite kinds of games. Have students determine the fractional probability that a student will like each type of game best. You may wish to provide students with copies of the Fun and Games Probability worksheet, on page 48, to use.

🌀 Try some playing-card probability. Have students work in small groups. Give each group a deck of playing cards. Ask the groups to solve these probability questions.

- What is the probability that you will pick a red card? a black card? a seven? a red seven? a seven of hearts?

Have students justify their answers in their math journals.

Fun and Games Glyph

1. Do you like to play card games?

	yes	no
cut a rectangle (w x h)	4" x 5"	3" x 4"

2. About how many days each week do you play video games?

	1	2	3	4	5	6	7	0
put this number in top left corner of card	1	2	3	4	5	6	7	8

3. Which type of game would you rather play?

	card game	ballgame	video game	board game
draw the above number of these in center of card	♡ hearts	◇ diamonds	♣ clubs	♠ spades

4. Do you prefer indoor or outdoor games?

	indoor	outdoor
Put the above number in bottom right of card?	yes	no

5. Does your favorite game require more luck or skill?

	luck	skill
color of border	green	blue

Now draw a picture of your favorite game on the back of your playing-card glyph.

1997 Good Apple

U.S. measurement

Fun and Games Glyph

1. Do you like to play card games?

	yes	no
cut a rectangle (w x h)	10.2 cm x 12.7 cm	7.6 cm x 10.2 cm

2. About how many days each week do you play video games?

	1	2	3	4	5	6	7	0
put this number in top left corner of card	1	2	3	4	5	6	7	8

3. Which type of game would you rather play?

	card game	ballgame	video game	board game
draw the above number of these in center of card	♡ hearts	◇ diamonds	♧ clubs	♤ spades

4. Do you prefer indoor or outdoor games?

	indoor	outdoor
Put the above number in bottom right of card?	yes	no

5. Does your favorite game require more luck or skill?

	luck	skill
color of border	green	blue

Now draw a picture of your favorite game on the back of your playing-card glyph.

Metric measurement

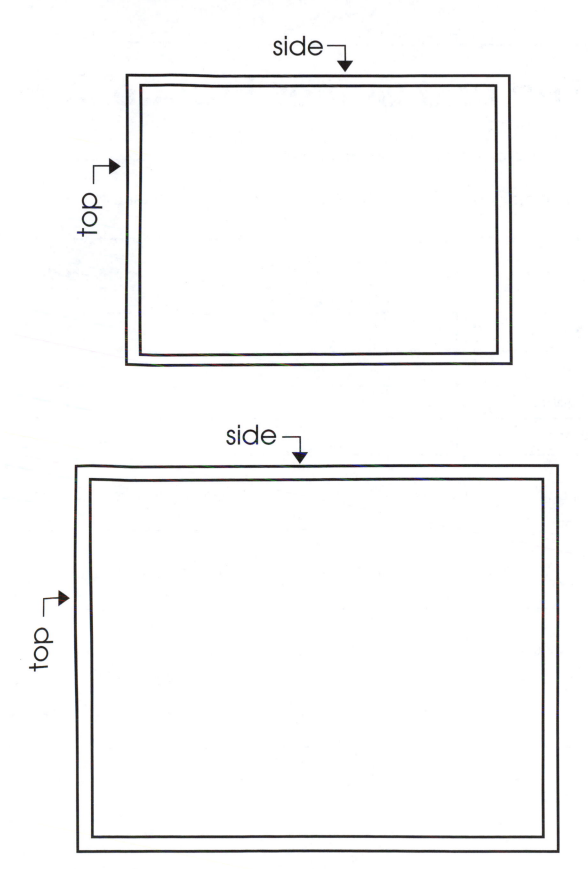

side ↓

top →

side ↓

top →

Measure and select the correct size playing-card pattern to complete the Fun and Games Glyph.

Fun and Games Probability

1. What is the total number of students in your class?_____

2. Use your class's data from survey question #3 to complete the table below.

game	number of students selecting game	fraction of class
card game		
ballgame		
video game		
board game		

3. Based on the data from your table, what is the probability that someone in your class likes to play video games best? _____

4. What is the probability that a student in your class likes to play card games best?

_____

5. If a new student joined your class tomorrow, which type of game do you think he or she would prefer? Use the data on the table to justify your answer. _____

_____

_____

_____

48

Shamrock Mobile Glyph

Many people like to wear green or orange on St. Patrick's Day. Invite students to create Shamrock Mobile Glyphs for St. Patrick's Day by answering the glyph's "green" survey questions and following the survey directions. To construct the glyphs, students cut out circles with specific diameters (see pattern on p. 52), and then cut crepe-paper streamers, attaching them to the circles to create this holiday mobile.

Materials

- glyph survey and directions
- shamrock pattern (copied on heavy paper)
- crepe-paper streamers, 1" wide by 9" long (2.5 cm by 23 cm)
- ruler
- crayons or markers
- scissors
- tape or glue
- paper and pencil (for activity below)
- string (for activity below)

Additional Activities

⊙ Challenge students to use the data from their glyphs to answer fraction problems such as the following.

- Determine the fraction of students in the class who are wearing something green today.

- What fraction of the class likes green beans best?

- What fraction of the girls in the class have green eyes?

- What fraction of the people wearing green like green beans best?

Encourage students to write a few fraction problems for their classmates to solve.

⊙ Attach strings to the tops of the glyphs. Display the glyphs by hanging them around the classroom.

Shamrock Mobile Glyph

1. Do you have green eyes?

	yes	no
design on shamrock	stripes	dots

2. Which is your favorite shade of green?

	kelly green	neon green	light (pastel) green
cut out the circle with a diameter of	5"	6"	7"

3. Are you wearing something green today?

	yes	no
color the shamrock	light green	dark green

4. Which is your favorite green vegetable?

	peas	green beans	broccoli	other
number of crepe-paper streamers	2	3	4	5

5. Which green candy do you prefer?

	green M&M's	green Lifesavers	green jellybeans	none
length of crepe-paper streamers	9"	8"	7"	6"

U.S. measurement

Shamrock Mobile Glyph

1. Do you have green eyes?

	yes	no
design on shamrock	stripes	dots

2. Which is your favorite shade of green?

	kelly green	neon green	light (pastel) green
cut out the circle with a diameter of	12.7 cm	15.2 cm	17.8 cm

3. Are you wearing something green today?

	yes	no
color the shamrock	light green	dark green

4. Which is your favorite green vegetable?

	peas	green beans	broccoli	other
number of crepe-paper streamers	2	3	4	5

5. Which green candy do you prefer?

	green M&M's	green Lifesavers	green jellybeans	none
length of crepe-paper streamers	22 cm	20 cm	17 cm	15 cm

Metric measurement

Weather Watchers Glyph

Using the newspaper to find weather data for various cities throughout the United States, invite students to create weather glyphs. You may wish to begin the lesson with a look at the weather section of the newspaper, pointing out the data on high and low temperatures and precipitation. Invite students to each select a city, locate the high and low temperatures for the day, and determine if there is any precipitation. Students can then begin creating their glyphs by using the reproducible cloud and sun pattern on page 55. Have students cut out the pattern following the glyph directions. (Advise students to outline the glyph pattern where they plan to cut it, then recheck their data before cutting.) Invite students to add the remaining details to their glyphs to show their answers to questions #2, 3, and 4.

Materials

❖ glyph survey-directions
❖ cloud pattern
❖ crayons or markers

❖ weather section of a newspaper
❖ basket (for activity below)
❖ paper and pencil (for activity below)

Additional Activities

⊚ Place glyphs in a basket. Ask each student to select one glyph from the basket and, using the data from the glyph, list the items he or she would pack if traveling to that city today. For example, if the weather is 50°F (10°C) and rainy, a student might list a jacket, blue jeans, a sweatshirt, and an umbrella. If it's 80°F (27°C) and sunny, the list might include shorts, a T-shirt, a tennis racket, and a bathing suit. Remind students to consider the daytime and evening temperatures when packing for their trips.

⊚ Ask students to gather data about the daily high and/or low temperatures in a city for a one-week period of time. Challenge them to create a line graph to show their data.

⊚ Invite students to research weather conditions for cities in other parts of the world. Have them create glyphs for these cities, then list items to include if their travel plans were to take them to those places.

Weather Watchers Glyph

1. What was the day's high temperature?

cut out the sun on this line	below 20°F	20°F–39°F	40°F–59°F	60°F–79°F	80°F or above
	below -7°C	-7°C–4°C	5°C–15°C	16°C–26°C	27°C or above
	1st line smallest sun	2nd line a little larger	3rd line even larger	4th line still larger	5th line largest sun

2. What was the day's low temperature?

draw this number of birds on the cloud	below 20°F	20°F–39°F	40°F–59°F	60°F–79°F	80°F or above
	below -7°C	-7°C–4°C	5°C–15°C	16°C–26°C	27°C or above
	0	1	2	3	4

3. What was the change in temperature for the day?

	0–15°	16–30°	31° or more
color of sun	red	orange	yellow

4. Was there any precipitation (rain, snow, hail)?

	yes	no
draw a lightening bolt on the cloud? 	yes	no

Play Ball! Glyph

Students may enjoy creating sports jersey glyphs by answering survey questions about their interest and participation in sports. The added shirt decorations will correspond to their survey answers.

Materials

- ❖ glyph survey-directions
- ❖ sports jersey pattern
- ❖ ruler
- ❖ crayons or markers
- ❖ pencil
- ❖ construction paper (for activity below)

- ❖ compass (for activity below)
- ❖ protractor (for activity below)
- ❖ A Circle of Sports worksheet, on page 59 (for activity below)
- ❖ Our Favorite Sports worksheet, on page 60 (for activity below)

Additional Activities

🌀 Provide students with copies of the A Circle of Sports worksheet. Ask each student to label and analyze a circle graph about his or her favorite sport.

🌀 For an extra challenge some students may be able to create authentic class circle graphs using data about the class's favorite sports. Invite each student to make a circle with a diameter of 8" (20 cm). Using ratios and the Our Favorite Sports worksheet, ask students to complete the graphs to show the data from their classmates' glyphs.

Teacher Note

You may wish to have students use calculators to compute the equivalent fractions in step #3 of the Our Favorite Sports worksheet.

Play Ball! Glyph

1. Do you like to watch sports on television?

	yes	no
stripe on sleeves?	yes	no

2. Would you rather play sports or watch someone else play?

	play	watch
name on shirt	last name	first name

3. Do you play on a sports team?

	yes	no
label front of shirt with number that is	even and a multiple of 3	odd and a multiple of 7

4. Have you ever gone to a professional sporting event?

	yes	no
write shirt number on sleeves too?	yes	no

5. What is your favorite sport?

	soccer	baseball or softball	basketball	other
color of shirt	yellow	purple	red	orange

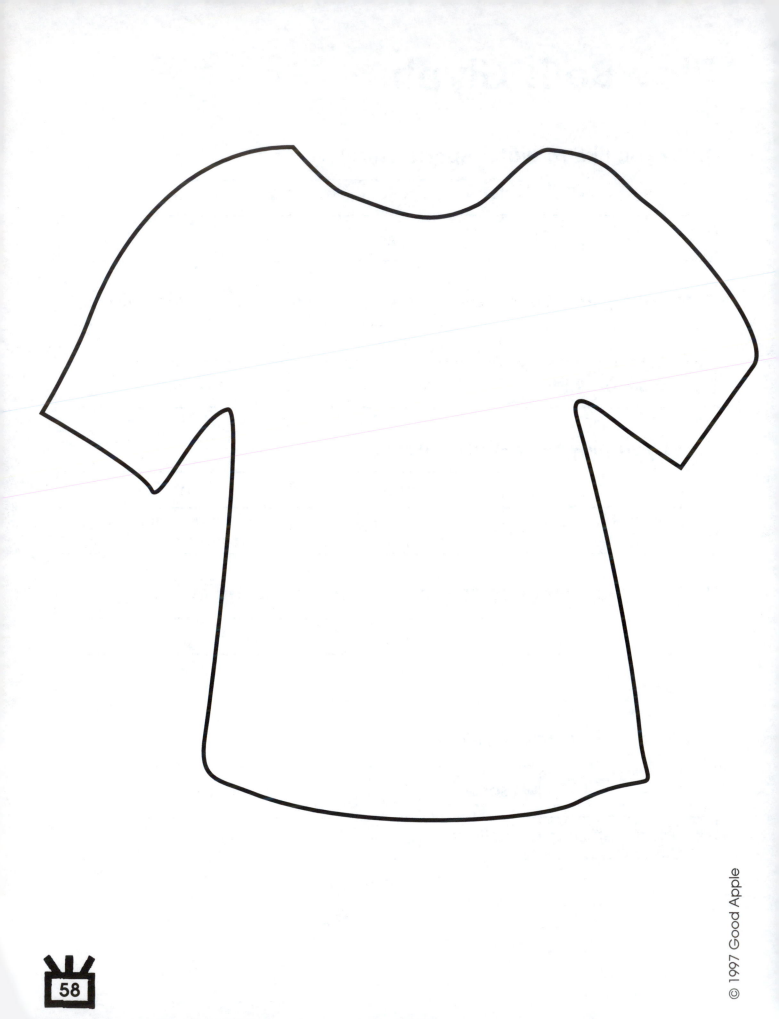

A Circle of Sports

1. There were 32 students in Mrs. Morley's class. Their favorite sports were

soccer	16
baseball or softball	4
basketball	8
other	4

2. Label each section of the circle graph below to show the data about students' favorite sports.

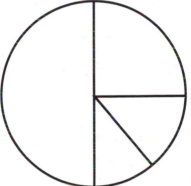

3. Explain how you knew which section of the graph represented the students who liked basketball best. _____

_____

_____

_____

4. Write a fraction that shows the part of the class that likes baseball or softball best. _____

5. Explain how you chose the numerator and denominator for your fraction.

_____

_____

_____

Name _____ Date _____

Our Favorite Sports

Create a circle graph using the data from your Play Ball! Glyphs.

1. Tally the favorite sports for students in your class, using the form below.

	Tally Total
soccer	
baseball or softball	
basketball	
other	

2. Show your class results in fraction form. (If 5 children out of 28 like soccer best, your fraction for soccer is $\frac{5}{28}$.)

Fraction of Class Who Chose Each Sport

Soccer   _____

Baseball or softball   _____

Basketball   _____

Other   _____

3. A circle is 360°. To create a circle graph, change each fraction to an equivalent fraction with a denominator of 360. These new fractions will help you figure out how much of the circle graph (a total of 360°) each sport should receive. Next to each fraction above, write the new equivalent fraction. *Check your work: The four numerators should add up to 360!*

4. Using a compass and another sheet of paper, construct a circle with a radius of 2" (5 cm). Use your protractor to measure out the four sections of the graph to match the equivalent fractions above. (If your fraction is $\frac{70}{360}$, make that section of your graph a 70° angle.) Be sure to label the sections of your graph and add a title to the graph.

60

Bookmark Glyph

Invite students to answer the survey questions on page 62 to create Bookmark Glyphs that show their reading habits. Because the bookmark glyph designs are abstract, it may be helpful to provide a sample for students to see before beginning construction work.

Materials

- ❖ glyph survey-directions
- ❖ bookmark pattern, traced or photocopied on heavy paper (construction paper or tagboard), or strips of heavy paper about 2 5/8" by 6 1/2" (6 cm by 16.5 cm)
- ❖ crayons or markers
- ❖ pencil
- ❖ scrap paper (for activity below)
- ❖ How Many Books Does Our Class Read in a Year? worksheet, on page 64 (for activity below)

Additional Activities

⑥ In creating their glyphs, students will have estimated the number of books they read in one month.

- Ask students to use this data to determine the approximate number of books they would read in one year.
- After students have calculated their yearly totals (in the activity above), ask each student to complete a stem-and-leaf plot, using copies of the worksheet on page 64, to show the entire class's data.

⑥ Ask students to use data from survey question #3 to find the class's mean, median, mode, and range.

Teacher Note

Before beginning the stem-and-leaf plot, you may wish to poll the class to determine the highest number of books read in one year. This information will allow students to add extra lines to the worksheet plot if there is a student whose data will not fit on the supplied form.

Bookmark Glyph

1. Where do you read more?

	school	home
add a border with	wavy lines	straight lines

2. Do you like to read in bed?

	yes		no	
divide bookmark lengthwise with a	wavy line		straight line	

3. About how many books do you read each month?

	0	1	2	3	4	5 . . .
number of circles	0	1	2	3	4	5 . . .

4. Of the following types of books, which would you rather read?

	mystery	biography	nonfiction	humor
number of triangles	1	2	3	4

5. How many times do you go to the library each month?

	0	1 or 2	3 or more
number of squares	0	1 or 2	3

Name _____ Date _____

How Many Books Does Our Class Read in a Year?

1. Using the data from question #3 on the glyph survey, estimate the number of books you read in one year. Explain how you got your answer.

_____

_____

_____

2. Compile the class's results and complete the stem-and-leaf plot below to show your class's data.

Books Read in One Year

stem	leaf
0	
1	
2	
3	
4	
5	
6	
7	
8	
9	
10	
11	
12	

3. What is the range of the number of books read by your classmates in one year? Explain how you know this.

_____

_____

_____

My Home Glyph

Invite students to create glyphs that represent information about their homes. Have them begin by choosing the correct shape of their glyphs by answering the first question. After adding the details to the glyphs, have students cut them out. Students may then enjoy working in groups to make community maps (see Additional Activities below).

Materials

- ❖ glyph survey-directions
- ❖ construction paper, pencil, ruler, scissors
- ❖ Community Map worksheet, on page 68 (for activity below)
- ❖ butcher paper or posterboard (for each group in the activity below)

- ❖ glue sticks (for activity below)
- ❖ crayons or markers (for activity below)
- ❖ ruler (for activity below)
- ❖ pen or pencil and math journal (for activity below)

Additional Activities

🌀 Have students work in small groups to create Community Maps using their home glyphs. Students may use butcher paper or posterboard, following the directions on page 68.

🌀 After the maps have been created, representatives from each group can share the group's map with the entire class. Students may be asked to write directions for traveling from one place to another on their map. They can be asked to write about why they selected the locations where they placed their houses. What factors affected their decision? They may be asked to write about what they would like to add to their community and why. Students can be asked to calculate the fraction of homes in their community that have pets, or the fraction of homes that have eight or more people living in them. Students can write about the strategies they used to answer these and other questions.

Teacher Note

When constructing rectangles or squares, advise students to begin at the corner of a piece of paper. Students can then measure and mark from each side to create the square or rectangle.

My Home Glyph

1. Do you live in a house, townhouse, apartment, or other type of home?

	house	townhouse	apartment	other type of home
size of glyph (width x height)	5" x 3"	3" x 5"	4" x 4"	4" x 3"

2. What is the outside of your home mostly made of?

	brick	wood	vinyl siding	other
shape of door	square	rectangle	triangle	pentagon

3. How many bedrooms are in your home?

	1	2	3	4 or more
number of windows	1	2	3	4

4. Do you have a fireplace?

	yes	no
shape of roof	trapezoid	triangle

5. How many people live in your home (including yourself)?

	2–4	5–7	8 or more
shade each window	$\frac{3}{4}$	$\frac{3}{8}$	$\frac{5}{8}$

6. Do any pets live with you?

	yes	no
doorknob on	right	left

U.S. measurement

66

© 1997 Good Apple

My Home Glyph

1. Do you live in a house, townhouse, apartment, or other type of home?

	house	townhouse	apartment	other type of home
size of glyph (width x height)	15 cm x 8 cm	8 cm x 15 cm	12 cm x 12 cm	12 cm x 8 cm

2. What is the outside of your home mostly made of?

	brick	wood	vinyl siding	other
shape of door	square	rectangle	triangle	pentagon

3. How many bedrooms are in your home?

	1	2	3	4 or more
number of windows	1	2	3	4

4. Do you have a fireplace?

	yes	no
shape of roof	trapezoid	triangle

5. How many people live in your home (including yourself)?

	2–4	5–7	8 or more
shade each window	$\frac{3}{4}$	$\frac{3}{8}$	$\frac{5}{8}$

6. Do any pets live with you?

	yes	no
doorknob on	right	left

Metric measurement

Community Map

1. Draw a compass rose on your map.

2. Decide on symbols and locations for the following items and place them on your map: a school, a library, a police station, a grocery store, a park, and a lake. Create a legend for your map.

3. Add a river and at least five roads to your map. Decide on names for the river and roads and label them.

4. Glue each group member's home on the map. Let each group member choose a location that appeals to him or her.

5. Decide on a name for your community and write it at the top of your map.

Answer the following questions.

1. Why did you choose to place your home where you did? _____

_____

_____

_____

2. If you could add one more thing to your community, what would it be? Why?

_____

_____

_____

_____

Super Sandwich Glyph

Invite students to create Super Sandwich Glyphs by answering questions about their favorite sandwich fillings. Have each student cut out a sandwich bun (see pattern on p. 72) and glue the bottom bun to a sheet of paper. Then, students may draw and color the layers of their sandwiches, based on their survey answers. Finally, students may glue the top buns onto their sandwiches.

Materials

- ❖ glyph survey-directions
- ❖ sandwich bun pattern
- ❖ paper (to glue bun onto; pastel-color paper works well)
- ❖ crayons or markers

- ❖ ruler
- ❖ scissors
- ❖ glue
- ❖ paper and pencil (for activity below)

Additional Activities

⦿ After they have created their glyphs, ask students to switch glyphs with a partner. Have students use rulers and glyph survey information to determine the favorite sandwiches of their partners.

⦿ Imagine that the class is having a special luncheon and each child will order the super sandwich he or she created. Have students tally the class's glyph information to determine the following.

- How many white rolls and how many whole-wheat rolls will be needed to make all the sandwiches?

- If rolls are only sold by the dozen, how many dozen of each type should be bought?

- If one tomato can be sliced and placed on four sandwiches, how many tomatoes will be needed for the class?

- If three tuna sandwiches can be made with each can of tuna, how many cans will be needed?

- If 1 pound (450 grams) of beef, turkey, or ham lunch meat will make eight sandwiches, how many pounds of each type of meat will be needed? Note: Lunch meat can be bought in 1/4-pound (112-gram) increments.

Super Sandwich Glyph

1. **Would you like to make your sandwich with white rolls or whole-wheat rolls?**

	white	whole-wheat
color of bun	white	brown

Cut out the bun. Glue the bottom bun to a piece of paper and begin to create your sandwich by drawing and coloring each layer.

2. **Which type of sandwich do you prefer?**

	ham	beef	turkey	tuna
add a blue layer with this thickness	$\frac{1}{4}$"	$\frac{1}{2}$"	$\frac{3}{4}$"	1"

3. **How much cheese would you like on your sandwich?**

	a lot	a little	none
add a yellow layer with this thickness	$\frac{1}{2}$"	$\frac{1}{4}$"	no yellow layer

4. **Do you want tomato slices on your sandwich?**

	yes	no
add a $\frac{1}{4}$"-thick red layer?	yes	no

5. **Do you want lettuce on your sandwich?**

	yes	no
add a $\frac{1}{4}$"-thick green layer?	yes	no

6. **Would you like mustard, mayonnaise, or ketchup on your sandwich?**

	mustard	mayonnaise	ketchup	nothing
number of seeds on the top bun	3	4	5	0

Now glue the top bun onto your super sandwich.

 U.S. measurement

70

Super Sandwich Glyph

1. Would you like to make your sandwich with white rolls or whole-wheat rolls?

	white	whole-wheat
color of bun	white	brown

Cut out the bun. Glue the bottom bun to a piece of paper and begin to create your sandwich by drawing and coloring each layer.

2. Which type of sandwich do you prefer?

	ham	beef	turkey	tuna
add a blue layer with this thickness	5 mm	10 mm	15 mm	20 mm

3. How much cheese would you like on your sandwich?

	a lot	a little	none
add a yellow layer with this thickness	10 mm	5 mm	no yellow layer

4. Do you want tomato slices on your sandwich?

	yes	no
add a 5 mm-thick red layer?	yes	no

5. Do you want lettuce on your sandwich?

	yes	no
add a 5 mm-thick green layer?	yes	no

6. Would you like mustard, mayonnaise, or ketchup on your sandwich?

	mustard	mayonnaise	ketchup	nothing
number of seeds on the top bun	3	4	5	0

Now glue the top bun onto your super sandwich.

Metric measurement

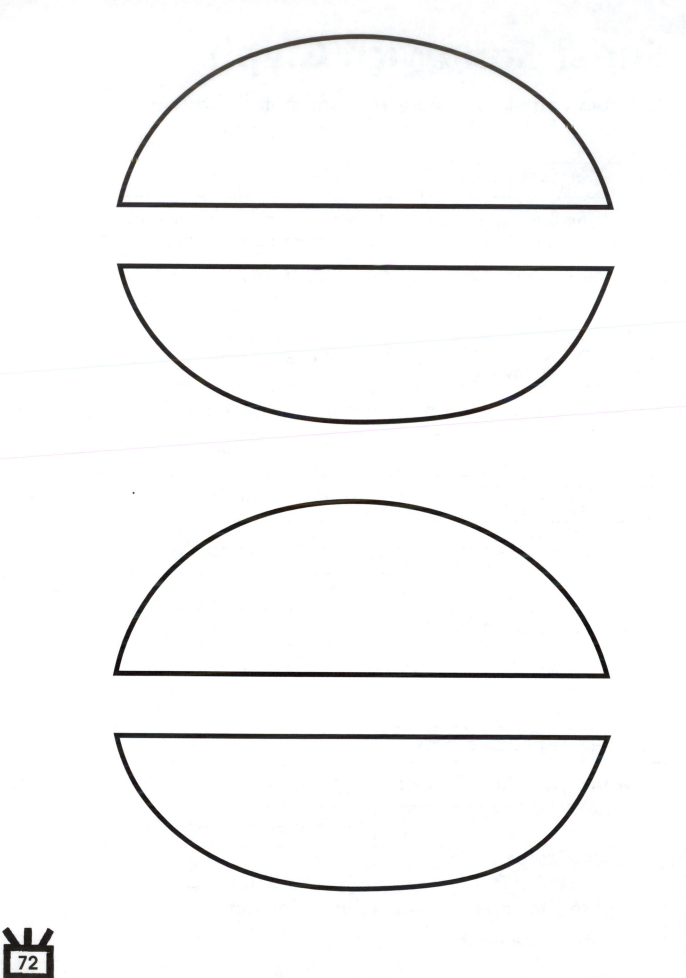

Postage Stamp Glyph

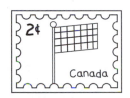

Invite students to monitor for one week the mail that arrives at their homes. Using the Mail Tally worksheet (see p. 76), have students keep a record of the types of items sent to their homes by mail. With the data they collect, they will be able to create Postage-Stamp Glyphs. Note: Parental assistance is encouraged, since students are asked to sort and record information about the family's mail.

Materials

❖ glyph survey-directions

❖ Mail Tally Worksheet, on page 76

❖ postage-stamp pattern

❖ crayons or markers

❖ paper, pen, and pencil (for activities below)

Additional Activities

🌀 Place students in groups of six. Ask groups to find answers to the following questions.

- Which group receives the most mail in one day? (Use the average amount of mail received each day.)

- Which group has the highest (or lowest) money value when their postage-stamp glyphs are added together?

🌀 Have students write a letter to local postal officials, telling them about the class glyph activity.

🌀 Research the cost of mail delivery in other countries. Design a table or graph to display the costs.

Postage Stamp Glyph

1. Did you receive more . . .

	bills	ads/ coupons	letters/ postcards	magazines/ catalogs	other
write the cost of the stamp on the glyph	1¢	2¢	3¢	4¢	5¢

2. Did you receive any magazines or catalogs this week?

	yes	no
written on stamp	Canada	United States

3. What is the average number of items you received each day?

	0	1	2	3	4	5	6 or more
color of border	green	blue	red	purple	brown	yellow	orange

4. When is your mail usually delivered?

	morning (before noon)	afternoon
design on the flag	intersecting lines	parallel lines

5. Do you enjoy getting mail?

	yes	no
top of flag pole		

74

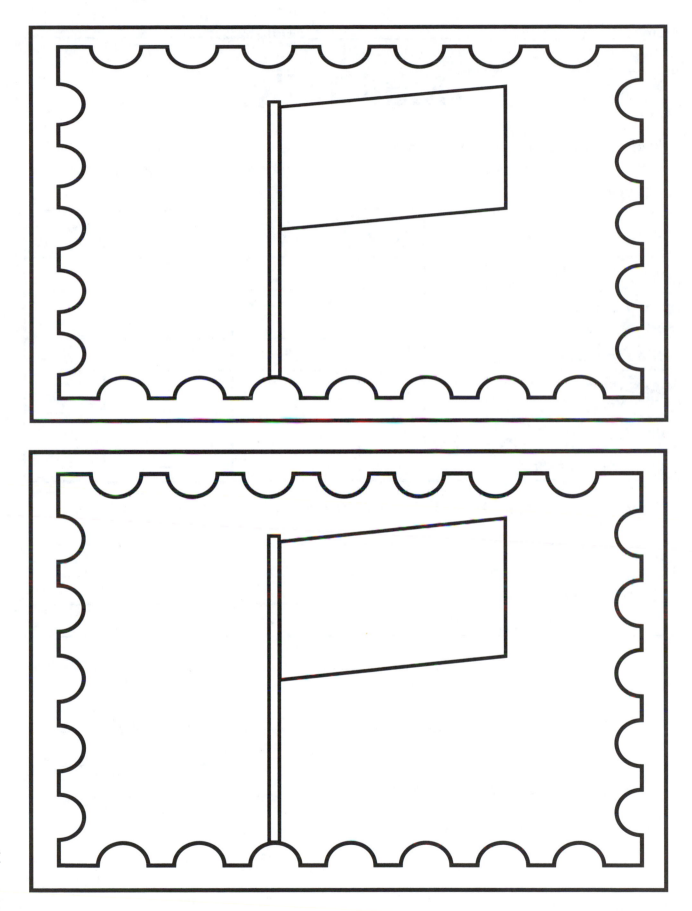

Mail Tally

1. Keep a record of all the mail delivered to your house in one week. Sort the mail into the following categories each day, and then record the number of pieces in each category in the table below.

	Day 1	Day 2	Day 3	Day 4	Day 5	Day 6	Weekly Total
bills							
advertisements/ coupons							
letters/postcards							
magazines/ catalogs							
other							
Total pieces of mail							

2. How many total pieces of mail were received at your house this week?

_____

3. What was the average amount of mail received at your house each day? _____
How did you figure this out? _____

_____

_____

_____

4. Which type of mail did you receive the most of during the past week? _____

_____

Which type of mail did you receive the least of? _____

_____

76

Deciding on the Survey Questions

Near the end of the school year, decide on some survey information that would lead to a discussion of the year. For example, you might ask students which assembly, field trip, or holiday party they liked best. Or ask students to select their favorite phys ed activity, song learned in music, recess activity, or science experiment. Students might select their favorite book-report project or school lunch. Choose questions that have two to five possible answers.

Deciding on the Glyph Attributes

Think about what the glyph will look like. Decide on a graphic or pattern (such as a star) and attributes (the shape, color, and facial features of the star). Assign each question a different attribute. See the sample on page 78 for possible ideas.

This is also the time to consider any skills you would like students to practice. Do you want them to measure lines or angles or recognize various shapes such as pentagons or octagons? If so, work these skills into your glyph design.

Materials

❖ glyph survey-directions

❖ other materials needed will be determined by your glyph directions

❖ paper, pencil, colorful construction paper, and tape (for activities below)

Additional Activities

⊚ Tally the results of each question to determine the class's favorites. Write a class letter to the incoming class (entering in the fall) telling them about the fun activities of the past school year. Save the glyphs and the letter to share with next year's class on the first day of school.

⊚ Glue each glyph to a colorful square of paper and tape the squares together to create a "Stars" quilt (for example, "Fifth-Grade Stars") that can be hung up in the classroom. Save the quilt for the beginning of the next school year, and have next year's students interpret the glyphs to find out information about this year's class.

Design Your Own School Year Memories Glyph

1. What was your favorite field trip?

	science center	museum
select a star with	pointed edges	rounded edges

2. Which assembly was your favorite?

	folk dancers	"Say No to Drugs"	spring concert
eyes	◕◔	◔◔	◔◕

3. Which book-report project did you enjoy most?

	diorama	poster	book jacket
nose	pentagon	hexagon	octagon

4. What was your favorite recess activity?

	kickball	jump-rope	soccer
add hair	X	X	⅄

5. What was your favorite phys ed activity?

	basketball	tumbling	dance
color of star	yellow	green	red

Add a mouth to show how you feel about moving to the next grade!

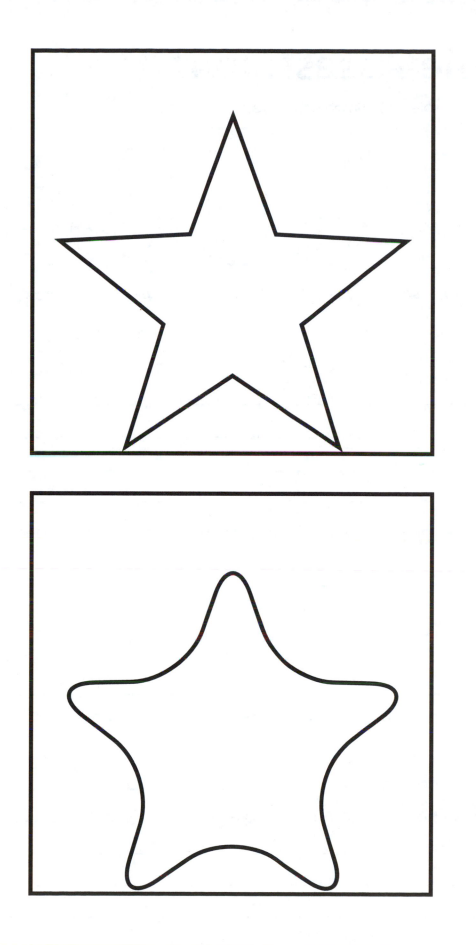

Sample Assessment

(based on the Bookmark Glyph on page 62)

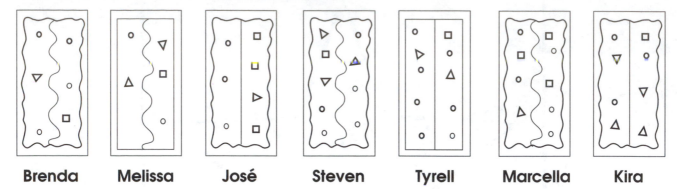

Brenda **Melissa** **José** **Steven** **Tyrell** **Marcella** **Kira**

Look at the Bookmark Glyphs shown above to answer the following questions.

1. Which students like to read in bed?_____

_____

2. Explain how you know this. _____

_____

_____

3. Complete the line plot to show about how many books these students read each month.

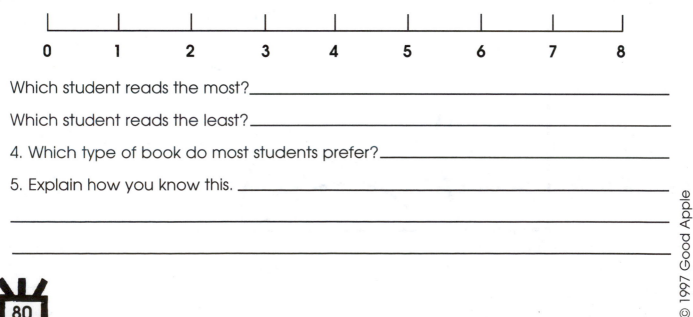

Which student reads the most?_____

Which student reads the least?_____

4. Which type of book do most students prefer?_____

5. Explain how you know this. _____

_____